THE ART OF SEEING

IN STREET PHOTOGRAPHY

Judith Farber

I dedicate this book to my Dad
(an amazing jazz drummer) who has
always been the biggest supporter of my
work, constantly reminding
me what a great photographer I am.
Thank you Dad. I love you.

And to all my students I've had
the pleasure of teaching!

Acknowledgements

My sincere thanks to the people who helped along the way to put this book together: Carole Merritt & Lara Reden (editing), Devon Farber (layout & design), Robert Farber, Blake Farber

CONTENTS

INTRODUCTION

There are a massive amount of books and websites about photography - composition, technical, color, black and white, critiquing photos, even the photographer's eye and mind. How do you choose? It comes down to the words and experiences from the author's personal perspective. This is my journey, which has embraced my heart with love and passion since the early 70's when I took my first workshop with Ansel Adams and Yousuf Karsh.

My specialty is teaching students how to see creating perfect framing on the streets. I am a huge proponent in learning how to frame an image with your eyes first. Feeling comfortable without a camera strengthens your eye. This prepares you to become faster and sharper with

1

camera in hand. When starting out I suggest perfecting the simplicity concept first and the power it has. Then adding other elements, so it all comes together for a successful outcome. For example, when you view a photo, does it evoke a feeling, how long do you stare at it, and can you relate. I don't believe in rules, but I do believe in perfecting the eye in how to see. By understanding the simple concepts in this book, your foundation will be formed. When layering that with further concepts, your style will emerge. I wrote this focusing on beginners who want a photographic eye. But I reach out to all levels. There's always something to learn. Practice with your camera so your personal style emerges. When you see something that excites you, gets your heart pumping, and if you can capture it successfully, you're on your way.

Living in New York City, life evolves around the streets, where there's a stimulating moment with each step. Images are made as we capture something that's forever changing. There's a situation that unfolds every minute. And it's finding the unexpected that excites my heart. As my favorite photographer, Henri Cartier Bresson once said (I quote him often):

Photography is nothing, it's life that interests me. Finding not only the light, but also the dark side of life energizes the passion that makes the search worthwhile.

In my classes I mention the Elements of Composition, helpful tips (not rules) to create a more cohesive style than what we might consider a dull, boring, snapshot (those endless travel or baby shots your friends make you sit through). My classes have been known to be a life-changing tool to jumpstart improvement in how your eye sees. I have often been asked about a handout on what's discussed. So here it is, plain and very simple. Find the words that resonate in creating the passion that triggers your unique personal vision.

Although it's not discussed here, don't forget the importance of being comfortable with your camera's functions. Through books, classes or websites, learn basic technical skills.

I hope you enjoy the craft as much as I enjoy teaching it.

Judith
January 2018, NYC

p.s. – I love critiquing your work. Readers of this book are eligible to receive a discounted one on one Private Image Critiquing Session, viewing online in real time your exercises from these assignments (or past work). Just email a photo of you holding this book.

ABOUT COMPOSITION

The dictionary refers to Composition as, *any work of art, from music to writing that is arranged or put together using conscious thought. The various visual elements, known as elements of design or elements of art (line, shape, color, texture, value, space) are the vocabulary with which the visual artist creates from. These elements relate to each other and to artwork as a whole.*

Composition in photography encompasses a similar format. There are various *Elements of Composition* that if perfected can produce a strong outcome. Capturing a style that reflects us personally is also part of the photographer's objective and goal. We bring our individual perspective into the frame, to comfort our own eye at the same time triggering, initiating and generating an emotion.

The Elements of Composition listed below will be discussed in more detail and applies to most photographic genres. Following each element are simple exercises (use images from the exercises for a one-on-one Critique Session with me, an enormously useful tool that instantly improves your eye and your photography).

1. Simplicity

2. Backgrounds

3. Leading lines

4. The Story

5. The Moments / Being Present

Street Photography is visual storytelling, taking people on our personal journey, recreating experiences from what we see into a pleasing replica within our camera's frame.

The challenge for most of us is what to include and what to eliminate. Understanding what a compelling subject is along with strong surrounding elements, and then knowing how to put it all together creates our photographic eye and an inspiring story.

As Ansel Adams once said, *You don't take a photograph, you make it.*

So the steps to composing goes something like this:

A moment of energy unfolds in front of you. Dissect the scene while keeping in the frame the most important parts of the whole, eliminating anything unrelated to a stronger story as distractions.

Using the implication of Ansel's quote, creating art is under our control. The main attraction (focal point) is what we include, while also our decision what to omit.

The Elements of Composition guidelines are steps to consider when framing a scene. Practicing and perfecting the steps most often will result in a stronger image.

Photography can leave us speechless. We experience new adventures and see for the first time, constantly testing our own creativity and imagination. We sense new vigor and fascination about people around the world, while at the same time turning us into amazing storytellers.

SIMPLICITY

Simplicity is an invaluable starting point for creating well-framed images. It's the easiest essential element to fine tune on the path to creating high-end photography.

Simplicity in photography means to keep to a minimum what's inside the frame. The more you photograph the more you understand the importance of singling out part of the whole from its surrounding, while leaving in that which has the most impact, the main attraction or focal point. This means keeping out clutter.

Capturing what your eye sees and your heart feels gives the viewer the best sense of your experience. The simpler the image, where the main focal point is obvious, translates into how easy the viewer is able to embrace your vision. It's also the fastest way to master good framing, looking for and including one person in the frame, one focal point. Seems simple right?

One Subject

If you enjoy photographing people, the easiest way to begin creating simplicity is to keep one subject within the frame; one focal point. Practice with finding one thing that catches your eye whether it's a shadow, a child in costume, an action shot.

Alone in Northern California

As in the example above, a man is sitting alone in contemplation at the beach on a foggy day. Note the simplicity of the photo. Does it instigate emotion? Is it relatable?

In Times Square, Cluttered vs Simplistic, keeping out distractions

Distractions

Omitting clutter keeps it simple. Clutter is anything in the viewfinder that doesn't add further strength to the main focal point. Make sure the viewfinder is void of distractions, including all four corners of the frame. The photo on the left is a typical busy crosswalk in NYC. It's not an interesting image since your eye is not fixed on any one focal point. With just a little patience, compare the image on the right taken just 2 minutes later using an angle that eliminates the clutter. There were a few people in front of the subject, however they were excluded resulting in a stronger, simplified image. You can avoid most clutter when your subject is singled out while also holding your camera at a diagonal (see Camera Angle below). Distractions and clutter can divert the eye away from the main focal point. The more distractions, the more the viewer could be left with a wandering eye searching for a focal point. While there is a place for clutter in photography down the road, when starting out keep one object of interest in as clear a path as possible.

Move in Closer

Another way to keep it simple is by cropping out distractions by moving in or zooming in closer to avoid them. For example, zooming in can capture the most interesting architectural detail of a an old building, the perfectly aligned row of colorful fall trees amid a pine forest, the eagle hovering over a flock of birds, the toddler giggling looking up at dad in Times Square, etc. Avoid distractions by moving in closer or zooming in (for the more advanced, common to delete various distractions, removing objects with post processing tools such as Adobe Photoshop or iPhone apps such as Snapseed or TouchRetouch).

Robert Capa once said, *If your photographs aren't good enough, you aren't close enough.***(1)** The power of an image often originates from its simplicity within the frame. A successful image can often by achieved by just getting in closer.

Asbury Park, NJ

Take the example above. On the left is a typical photo of a summer beach day. By moving in closer, there are more options of interest to single out (ok, he looks like he's peeing, and why I took it). Zooming in keeps the overall photo more simplistic with an obvious and clear focal point. Easy right?

Bethesda Terrace, Central Park

The Central Park photo is a different scenario. The photo on the left shows a uniformed man heading up the stairs. It's a simple photo that works well with our discussion on one main focal point with no distractions. The version on the right was taken 5 seconds later showing two people who entered the frame. This is an example of not only needing to be quick on the shutter but also where both photos work as simplistic. Do you see why?

The one on the right is simple because of a comfortable balance to our eye, with no other distractions and the timing of hitting the shutter at the perfect moment. The people on either side of the uniformed man are of equal distance apart while also similarly half cut out of the frame, forming a diagonal line. This is an example of a photo that has simplicity with balance and no distractions. What's left in the photo adds to the final story without detracting from the main focal point. Clutter might interfere with the crucial moment or story while for each individual circumstance is controlled by camera angle, patience or even removal.

Camera Angle

By simply changing the camera angle can also create simplicity. The most commonly used angle is the horizontal. As important as this angle is for storytelling or capturing scenic landscapes, the horizontal angle tends to include extraneous information on its sides, which could lessen the photo's impact and strength. Assess the scene, and pick the best angle. As elementary as choosing the right angle might seem, it's surprising how many stick to the same angle or choose the wrong one. This is a common mistake my students often make. If your scene is wide, horizontal is the practical choice. If there are distractions surrounding your subject on the sides, try a vertical, which might remove them. If the scene has height, i.e. tall buildings, trees with a moonlit sky, then vertical would be the likely choice.

The diagonal angle keeps out distractions adding energy and feeling of movement,similar to the Times Square example.

My favorite angle, which I've discussed and new to many but used the least, is the diagonal. Here your camera is held tilted, halfway between a horizontal and a vertical (see example above). Use this angle when a subject is closely surrounded by distractions on two sides. The stairs in this photo above are obviously showing as diagonal, but the image works even though our mind thinks she'd better hold on not to slide down. The viewer might feel off guard viewing a diagonal image, while often it looks great for stronger impact. I suggest trying it, diagonals are always fun.

I recommend studying the subject and background then adjusting to the proper angle. Experiment with each angle. Spend time doing verticals, horizontals, and diagonals. Perhaps create an inspiring project around the new angle. Doing the exercises will result in a new way of seeing, you'll become faster in choosing the right angle, resulting in a clearer understanding of which one works best for which scene.

Quick on the Shutter

Street photography involves two opposing attributes: being quick and being patient.

A powerfully dramatic moment could be a challenge to capture if you are not quick enough. How you frame the scene, deciding what to include and what to leave out is best accomplished in a split second.

Try this assignment: Locate a moving subject (car, jogger, kids running, etc). Angle your camera correctly to avoid as many distractions as you can. Count the seconds it takes from seeing an enticing scene, bringing your camera from hip to eye, choosing the angle, clicking the shutter and capturing the moment. How long did that take? Was it more than 10 seconds? Your goal is 6! Moments are gone in less time than that. Practice being quick on the shutter! The more you do, the quicker you'll get.

Slow Down

We need to become fast on the shutter, while also having patience to search for perfect moments, and patience waiting for crowds to disburse. Having patience and being quick on the shutter are indispensable. Looking out for an interesting moment becomes clearer when we slow ourselves down. Photography can manifest calm. Our state of emotion reflects how we see and what we shoot. We observe more when we're calm, no matter how crazy or crowded the location might be.

Creating simplicity in camera can be achieved anywhere from Times Square, the streets of Hong Kong, 5th Ave on Christmas Eve, the Redwood Forest, to the beaches of Waikiki. It's all about your position, how you angle your camera while being quick on the shutter.

Taken from a boat on the Bangkok canal

The photo above was shot on a slow moving boat on a crowded canal in Bangkok. I noticed what could be a great shot in the distance, a man sitting alone, staring. But I also had to be quick, knowing the scene will disappear fast. I held up my camera zooming in to crop out side distractions. I knew it was a horizontal since it had room on either side to add strength to include a sense of place. I keep it simple and uncomplicated, and (with patience) waited for a clearer view from passing boats. Then it's quick on the shutter before I was too far away and he was completely out of sight. This process needs to happen within 5 seconds or the shot could be lost. Practice is key!!

How much you see around you, how you hold your camera, how fast you are on the shutter, how you crop out distractions, how calm you remain, all combined can produce a magnificent shot. I believe I would not have created my favorite images if I did not understand these concepts. With every step, slow yourself down, take a deep breath, look around, find and frame a masterpiece. For there's one found with every step you take.

Visual Arts

There's a correlation between simplicity and various visual art forms such as film, paintings, stage/theatre design, architecture, interior design, etc.

An observable approach to understanding framing is to study filmmakers, artists and photographer's works. Dissect the images and their impact, the subject, angles chosen, the simplicity factor, distractions and balance.

The goal is to have your images stand on their own, telling a story. Thinking this way, your eye will begin to change, opening up your vision to what's around you, while at the same time understanding how powerfully effective framing is.

The impact you create with your camera is within your control. What you keep in the frame and what you omit is your choice. Whatever has the most emotional charge stays, and what doesn't is omitted by camera angle, getting closer or excuse the expression...post processing!

Many words to say one thing: **KEEP IT SIMPLE!**

Review

1. Find one subject, point of interest, scene, graphic that moves you
2. Remove unnecessary distractions so the scene remains simple
3. Get in close. If intimidated, use a telephoto lens, not to affect the moment
4. Consider the angle that communicates your vision - vertical, horizontal or diagonal. Search for the best viewpoint, high, low or eye level for impact and drama
5. For people photography, practice being quick on the shutter
6. Slow down, think patience waiting for less distractions or a special moment
7. Study artists' works and simple frames in films

Assignment

Photograph one intriguing subject. Study the subject and adjust to the proper angle. Take three different photos experimenting with verticals, horizontals and diagonals.

Go to your local bookstore's art/photography section (or a Museum). Observe your favorite artist and photographer's work noticing the angle chosen and simplicity of the piece.

(1) http://www.magnumphotos.com/C.aspx?VP3 =CMS3&VF=MAGO31_9_VForm&ERID=24KL 535353

(2) **The Minds Eye**, 1999: Texts by Henri Cartier-Bresson. Aperture, New York. Decisive Moment, page 20

BACKGROUNDS

A background in photography is what fills the frame around the main focal point. It's equal in importance to the subject. Think about the background as yet another subject. We tend to focus on the subject alone and often ignore what is behind or surrounding it. For street photography, a background is crucial and could be anything from a solid colored wall, a storefront, a city view, window, columns, the forest, a sunset, a meandering path, crowds or even a blur, etc. I am always on the lookout for a great background to complement and strengthen the impact of my main subject.

As the subject is crucial, the background is also half the photo too. Locate one of interest. One that is unique. Concentrate on a section in the background that will not cause further distractions, just by moving your position and camera angle. Perhaps the simplest part works best, so as not to detract from but to enhance the subject, adding a sense of place.

A neutral background keeps the focus on the elderly Miao woman. Taken at a mountain village outside Sanya, Hainan Island, China

A simple way to locate a good background is when you find one that is neutral. Neutrality in a background refers to placing your main focal point or subject in front of something that is of a neutral setting. This can be as simple as a solid colored wall (above example) to more complex repetitive patterns. By patterns

I mean an arrangement in design that are continuous and equally spaced apart, such as bricks, tiles, circles, stripes, plaids, stairs as repetitive horizontals, columns as repetitive verticals (see next photo), exterior façade that has a repetitive design, even a fence. Since these patterns repeat themselves, they feel neutral to the eye and create a simplistic but compelling background.

Repetitive vertical columns lined up can be neutral to our eye. Stand where they are evenly spaced apart while avoiding distractions in its open spaces

Above is an example of a background considered neutral. Why? Because the columns are vertically lined up, evenly spaced apart, repetitive and therefore, neutral to our eye. To have them evenly spaced, find the exact place to stand where the columns have less or equal space between them. Evenly spaced is key in keeping the background simple, while not allowing distractions between its open spaces. Always move around and experiment with different angles to locate that key place where they are lined up evenly.

How you angle the camera, where your subject is in relation to the background, and where you stand can make or break a good background. You want the background to give a sense of neutrality where the subject stands out. And as you can see, it doesn't have to be a plain solid wall.

Sometimes it takes a little experimentation to find the perfect spot to stand to achieve the best neutral background. With a little patience, awareness of the background, finding the best place to stand for the simplest background, plus timing, all the elements come together. When you locate a great background, set up the framing first (vertical/ horizontal), so when crowds disperse you're ready to click the shutter. Now you are creating an environmental portrait, finding the perfect background while keeping the subject as the main focal point.

Where the subject is placed will affect a busy background. In Queens, NY, since the 1990's the 5 Pointz Warehouse was a graffiti ridden art space for 1500 artists. Sadly demolished to give way to a high-rise apartment building

As mentioned, backgrounds do not have to be boring to be neutral. Graffiti is a fine example of a busy background with the challenge of the subject to stand apart. Where the subject is placed will impact the final affect. In the example above, the subject was in the darker section, which enabled her to stand out. A piece of art can create a feeling of neutrality, while at the same time the subject authenticates the art's size and scale.

Blurred background

A blurred effect makes a cluttered background fade, allowing the subject to stand out. A busy background, or one strong in color might distract from the subject. If you have a camera that manually adjusts, use a lower aperture (f-stop number) such as f4 to blur a cluttered background. If the background is crucial to the final image, use a higher f-stop such as f11 or f16 to keep the background more in focus. Beware of obstructions in the background that distract your eye away from the subject, either move your position or blur the background with your settings.

Blurred background lessens its importance

Honey Boy's final run at the beach, background not
in focus

Story and Background

A background is crucial when telling a story, as it tells part of the narrative. Both the subject and background work together in a story, from an emotional level or for informational purposes.

Captions with story telling are great for revealing details and in photojournalistic pieces. Photos standing alone are successful when the image divulges, reveals or exposes something emotional, physical or spiritual to the viewer.

A background enhances a photo by contributing to its storyline. It represents a sense of place by providing more strength to the subject merely by fading away. Decide what will increase the photo's impact, and always frame it at the best angle to complement the subject. A lot of composing involves practice.

I work from awkwardness. By that I mean I don't like to arrange things. If I stand in front of something, instead of arranging it, I arrange myself. - Diane Arbus (1)

The Tibetan woman turned around just after reading about the NY hunger strike that affected her people. Photographed in Dharmasala, India

Review

1. Understand neutral in finding a great background, anything from a plain wall to patterns and textures that repeat themselves can be neutral to our eye

2. Notice how the background changes as you move.

3. Blurring can make a distracting background fade

4. The power of a complementary background when telling a story. For ex: the girl's excitement in a toy store, a bride and groom on a meandering path, a teen assisting an elderly man down the street.

Assignment

Walk your town/city/neighborhood and find interesting backgrounds. For example: repetitive verticals (similar structures lined up such as columns, fences), horizontals (stairs), shadows, crowds, trees, geometric patterns, architectural details, murals, etc. Look out and wait for the perfect subject to walk by.

(1) From the book, Diane Arbus, 1972, pg 12

LEADING LINES

Leading lines are any line or form of lines that lead your eye to a focal point. A leading line becomes an anchor within a frame, a point of strength that has a beginning and an end. The lines also add energy to an image and are often a distinct dynamic element.

There is a limitless amount of leading lines around us, for example, stair railings, meandering paths, fences, crosswalks, trees lined up, railroad tracks, etc. In other words, they're everywhere. You just have to open your eyes to find them.

Leading lines can be as subtle as a curb meeting the street or as obvious as the white lines in a crosswalk. When searching for leading lines look for something continuous that flows up, down, curved or diagonal.

Ultimately, you want the lines to lead to a specific focal point of interest. The type of the line is not important. It's just a line to direct your eye in a specific direction. The subject can also be placed anywhere along the line. However, the further back on the line the subject is, the more dynamic the photo might be, leading your eye towards an end point. The strength of a photo is even further pronounced if you frame the leading line to begin at one of the corners, ending at the opposite corner.

My class loves this exercise, being on the look out for leading lines. You will be amazed at you how many leading lines there are out there, while excited about something you've never noticed before. And when you do, it's all you'll see. Leading lines are another crucial tool for opening your eyes and expanding your vision. Your goal as a photographer is to observe and be aware of your surroundings. The best way to recognize leading lines is to view examples.

Leading lines can lead your eye through the image to a focal point, which happens to be my brother, Robby in Todos Santos, Baja, Mexico.

The stairs create more energy with a diagonal starting from the lower left corner leading your eye up to
the subject.

Double leading lines that meet can create an arrow affect of movement

Opposing leading lines as a perspective leads your eye down to the subject, creating an effect similar to railroad tracks

Cars lined up create a leading line from corner to corner

Leading lines can be a railing, ramp or staircase, leading your eye to the subject

Leading lines can be circular, while stronger when they begin in one corner and end in the opposite one

Review

1. Leading lines are anchors in a photo with a beginning and an end

2. Leading lines can be subtle or strong

3. Leading lines can lead the eye to a specific focal point of interest

4. Leading lines are strengthened when they begin in one corner leading the eye to the opposite corner

Assignment

Capture a leading line that begins in one corner and angling the camera so that the line ends at the opposite corner. Look for multiple leading lines, angling the camera in a way that captures the lines either as a perspective, as in railroad tracks or as parallel lines.

THE STORY

Telling a story with eye-catching photographs engages the audience. It creates a memory that holds a place in our hearts. When creating a story, being fully present in capturing a moment is essential. Photographing with impact can tell a story without captions. Choose a themed photojournalistic photo essay or just a one-photograph story. Either way, the stronger the photograph the stronger it can stand on it's own. Here we will discuss a story, creating images without captions.

When searching for a direction/style, where your passion lies, ask yourself some poignant questions:

1. *What do I love to photograph?*
2. *What compels, excites and inspires me?*
3. *What is my eye drawn to?*

4. *Is there a common thread or similar theme in my photography?*

This is a starting point when looking for a direction. I suggest writing your thoughts and ideas for more clarity. Then expand them further being aware of any recurring theme, purpose or insight that resonates.

Need inspiration? Hang out in a bookstore's art/photo section, view magazines that inspire (subscription and/or online): *Photolife, American Photo, Black & White, Aperture, National Geographic, Blur, Shadow and Light, Street Photography International,* etc. Watch documentary broadcasts on PBS, 60 Minutes and Vice for inspiration to spark ideas. There are an infinite number of resources.

Is your preference to photograph a one-image story or a series? One photo can tell a story just as much as a series, as long as it originates from your heart.

Once you have a theme, research your topic thoroughly. The more you know, the clearer your direction.

1. *Plan on either black and white or all color. Choose one for consistency and cohesiveness.*

2. *Will you interview subjects or prefer photographing from afar as the moment arises? While some photographers choose one on one interaction, you might be more comfortable capturing from afar. Whatever you decide use the appropriate lens for the job.*

If you interact with strangers, it gets easier as you go along. Having a project to work on is the perfect motive for talking to strangers. Engage in conversation about your project and show examples of your work. People are more open to being photographed when they feel comfortable with you, your passion for a topic, while being a part of something important. Your approach is critical. If it's a vendor buy something, and always offer to send photos. How approachable you are will determine how involved your subject will be. Just be mindful and respectful of all people on the street at all times. Be aware that some cultures and communities dislike having their photo taken.

The next tip is being quick on the shutter. As discussed, the more you shoot the quicker you become at not missing moments. When you find what could be an amazing shot, be prepared to capture it quickly. It's odd how my mind can still visualize photos that got away from not being quick enough on the shutter. Practice!

Know your camera's settings. Missing the story because you are fussing with settings is just plain frustrating. Know your camera's capabilities. The type of camera is not important, just be familiar with whatever format you are using. Perhaps it's time to refresh your skills with a technical session or a composition course for inspiration in framing.

If it's a photo documentary series or one shot, look for moments that keep our attention. When the viewer lingers on your photo, you got 'em! A good story results in imagining, reflecting and dreaming. Great images spark inspiration while others create yawns. Don't create yawns!

Compose your images to perfection. Reread earlier chapters on Simplicity, Background and Leading Lines. Composition is a combination of scale, external conditions, light, viewpoint/perspective, emotional impact along with a strong connection to the subject. How you compose is crucial. When you feel it all comes together, the story will be appreciated and worth sharing.

The more you shoot, the better you'll become at finding and capturing moments before they disappear. Let your eye and your heart be your guide. Your inner voice and intuition remain your strength along with your awareness in locating interesting moments in time. The more you practice the more your instinct takes over. Think back when your attention was drawn to something happening on the street where you pointed it out by saying, *hey look at that?* That's the moment you want to capture, and quickly!

Below are examples of a one-photo story without words. Notice how and why the photo stands out on its own.

There shouldn't be any captions. People should just look. We should awaken our sensitivity. – Henri Cartier-Bresson (1)

50 THE ART OF SEEING

©Henri Cartier Bresson   ©Sara Moon   ©Diane Arbus   ©Dorothea Lange

Viewing famous photographers' work (photo books, websites, movie frames, museums) all contribute to understanding what an effective photo story looks like. I suggest singling out what your eye is drawn to, analyzing the point of interest, the background, composition, leading lines, etc., and how the elements come together to create the overall strength and a successful storyline.

Sometimes it happens, the viewer isn't feeling what you felt. Perhaps they found something entirely different. They created their own story in their head, or saw nothing and you are left to explain your photo. Has this ever happened? Interpretations vary. Sometimes captions are essential if you want your story to come alive as you created it. It puts into context what the camera was not able to illustrate alone. Unless it's a photojournalistic piece, I do find the most memorable photos are those that speak without words. Ideally images stand on their own, telling a non-verbal story.

Imagine creating a scene similar to a movie frame, where the composition and the lighting come together and engage the senses. Henri Cartier-Bresson said, *"From some of the great films I learned to look, and to see."* (2). Think of your favorite films. Notice how each frame tells its story. Movies such as *Life*

of Pi (Claudio Miranda), *The Wizard of Oz* (Harold Rosson), *Lord of the Rings* (Andrew Lesnie), *Gone With The Wind* (Ernest Haller), *Mad Max* (John Seale), etc. The scenes were expertly planned where each frame was pure perfection. Thinking this way, your eye will begin to expand, while understanding the power of framing when telling a story with or without words.

Review

1. Good story telling originates from a unique perspective using great composition.

2. Use consistency in themes and a powerful image for single shot (without a caption)

3. Be quick on the shutter not to miss the moment

4. Know your camera and its settings

5. Your inner voice and intuition remain your strength in locating special moments in time

6. Study and dissect the composition of great photos, paintings and movie frames

Assignment

Choose a theme of interest and use photos (1- 10 images) to tell a powerful story without captions.

(1) <u>The Minds Eye,</u> 1999: Text by Henri Cartier-Bresson. Aperture, New York. Decisive Moment pg 20.

(2) *The Decisive Moment* from <u>The Mind's Eye</u>, *Writings on Photographs & Photographers* Text by Henri Cartier-Bresson. Aperture, New York. Decisive Moment, 1952

http://photohelios-team.blogspot.com/2009/02/essay-henri-cartier-bresson-1952.html

BEING PRESENT

The camera was invented to record images with the use of light. While appreciating the camera's historical impact on our lives, it warrants respect for another unspoken advantage.

Teaching photography is congruent with my background in studying mindfulness, where the idea of being present living in the now is key. Meditation is one tool that puts us in a calm state of presence, with appreciation and gratitude. Basically a mind/body check of where we are at this exact moment.

Street photography constantly reminds us to be present with the awareness of capturing moments. One evening while listening to a talk by a favorite Buddhist teacher, Jack Kornfield (Spirit Rock-California) I was especially impressed by what he said. He was describing the importance of being present through meditation. I love street photography and realized one reason I do is because it keeps my awareness in the present moment. So it seems *living in the now* has yet another tool, the camera.

Mindfulness is the capacity to be fully present for the experience of life, with a balance of open heart, open mind. -Jack Kornfield (1). Meditation teaches mindfulness, clearing distractions in your head while focusing on the breath to slow the mind. If you venture out on a meditative journey the tendency is to appreciate life's moments and gain the awareness of living in the now.

In my classes I mention keeping what's within the frame simple, removing distractions that do not add further strength to your subject. It's on the streets where we capture the simple moments that constantly keep us present.

One of my past students experienced an *aha* moment at the end of class after my discussion comparing street photography and mindfulness.

I learned so much today. I feel freer. Living mindfully, keeping it simple, focusing on removing distractions, seems to slow me down. I bet there could be significant improvement in my life if my focus remains strong enough. For this learning to become more present and aware could bring me to a new kind of freedom, perhaps even making it easier no matter what life stressors come my way. CL

Street photographer Henri Cartier-Bresson spoke of the decisive moments in photography, establishing this as a mainstream belief for street photographers.

Of all the means of expression, photography is the only one that fixes a precise moment in time. We play with subjects that disappear; and when they're gone, it's impossible to bring them back to life... - Henri Cartier-Bresson (2)

Photography is a drawing, done with intuition and you can't correct it. If you have to correct it, it's the next picture. But life is very fluid. You can't tell a person to smile again. Life is once, forever. – Henri Cartier-Bresson (3)

People watching is a leisure activity around the world. The reason it is so compelling is that it keeps us in the forever changing present moment. France practically ordained this as a marketable activity, the art of sitting at an outdoor café. It's enthralling and captivating all at the same time because we experience every type of emotion. Likewise, there's always something to observe and experience on the street, it's always changing and rarely boring.

An abundance of life's stories are told when we slow ourselves down and savor moments instead of rushing. With life's pressures, our minds are jammed full and often we forget to enjoy the ride. I especially love city life as it breeds an environment of endless interactions with strangers, always keeping us present. Those inspiring 2-minute conversations on the street captured without a camera are also truly treasured. The most passionate times are not often photographed. It's about the visual that remains in the mind's eye and adds to our memory.

Now is an adventure in not knowing. You have to be willing to get lost in the moment and let life take you from one moment to the next without knowing where it's taking you. The truth is that we never actually know what the next moment holds. - Gina Lake *(4)*

Photographing on the street can be a metaphor for our existence. When we experience a present moment unfolding, we are capturing something outside ourselves. It's a constant reminder that we are alive.

After teaching thousands of students, I recognize how street photography has the capacity to changes lives. Students find inspiration and delve deep inside to bond with their creative center, opening their vision, discovering *how to see* for the first time, or just appreciating the camera's hidden power in keeping us present. It's a simple reminder of the existence of that part of ourselves we rarely tap into.

I enjoy shooting a picture. Being present. It's a way of saying, "Yes! Yes! Yes! And there are no maybes. All the maybes should go to the trash, because it's an instant, it's a moment, it's there. - Henri Cartier-Bresson (5)

When photographing on the street one must be in touch within in order to capture what's outside. This enables us to experience fleeting moments. To be a successful street photographer is to be open to life as it is unfolding, constantly reminding us to be present without missing a beat whether it's down the street, around the corner or right in front of our noses.

An evening in a nearby café at Lake Como, Italy. She was joyfully and freely dancing in front of a church

On a stone ramp at a mosque in Istanbul, a glass partition preserved the ruins. He seemed captivated by what was behind the glass

A split second captured moment

Review

1. Being fully present is living in the now, an awareness around you

2. Being present in street photography is an awareness around you that is crucial in order to capture special moments.

3. An example of being present is people watching

4. Savor the moments with or without a camera.

5. Capturing something outside ourselves, a crucial moment is a reminder that we are in the present and alive.

Assignment

To test *living in the moment*, walk your neighborhood without a camera. Being observant is key. Notice everything. Being present and finding inspiration is a fun experiment without a camera. See how many moments there are to capture. Don't forget to look behind you.

Next time bring your camera walking the same area but this time taking quick photos of what your eye is drawn to.

What feels different? Are you able to find more inspiration with or without a camera? Does the camera offer inspiration or is it a hindrance? If it is a hindrance, the next step is to become more comfortable on the street with your camera. Feel it more as a body part, while at the same time practicing being quick on the shutter. When you can capture those moments with your camera that inspire, congratulations! You're in the moment and ready to create incredible stories.

(1) The Wise Heart *A Guide to the Universal Teachings of Buddhist Psychology* by Jack Kornfield, 2009

(2) American Photo, Henri Cartier-Bresson, September/October 1997, page: 76

(3*) There Are No Maybes' THE NEW YORK TIMES* Interview with Henri Cartier-Bresson by Sheila Turner-Seed - 1971

http://lens.blogs.nytimes.com/2013/06/21/cartier -bresson-there-are-no-maybes/?_r=0

(4) *How to Quiet the Mind* by Gina Lake, http://www .dailyom.com/cgi-bin/courses/courseoverview.cgi? cid=144

(5) *There Are No Maybes' THE NEW YORK TIMES* Interview with Henri Cartier-Bresson by Sheila Turner -Seed – 1971

http://lens.blogs.nytimes.com/2013/06/21/cartier -bresson-there-are-no-maybes/?_r=0

CRITIQUES

A photo critique is part of the learning process in photography, and often the subject of confusion. I want to clarify what critiquing is, its benefits and how you become proficient at doing a critique and the value of receiving one. Having a more in depth understanding of the process will open your eyes to a new way of seeing, improve how you photograph and view your images. The more you experience a critique the more powerful your own images become.

What Is A Photo Critique

A photo critique is where images are reviewed in detail for artistic and technical growth. Insightful, straightforward comments on your photo's strengths and weaknesses are offered with positive encouragement.

A critique is not a criticism. For many, images are personal. There is no place in critiques for nastiness, egotism or photo bashing. This can certainly damage one's self esteem. The photographer is seeking to advance with inspiring, in-depth encouraging discussions.

During my critiques we view images in real time. The photographer hears what their photos communicate emotionally, technically and creatively. Discussed are tools that further enhance the images. Hearing repetitive comments can elevate your skill level as you recognize exactly what you need to do to improve. The critique's value is to create photos with more impact while acquiring self-editing skills. The techniques learned alters the scope of what you see the next time you pick up your camera. Often a style emerges during a session, a common theme that ties your photos together. It then becomes apparent what your eye is drawn to. Besides this new learned skill, you leave feeling inspired, perhaps pursuing a new direction, reviving a passion, even finding your style.

Being Critiqued

There are a couple of ways to receive a critique. Photos can be emailed to a professional for written feedback, or in my sessions, viewed online in real time as we speak. Either way is beneficial. What I find distinguishable about my critiques is how a live session reveals that first impression while hearing stories of the photo's origin. A critique is also effective before a Portfolio Review. These are held at various cities with feedback from industry experts, helpful for assignments, meeting gallery directors, museum curators and book publishers.

Listening to feedback might be challenging, as we often feel connected to our work. Keep in mind comments are subjective. To achieve the ultimate outcome, be open, and do not feel as though it's a personal attack. It's about having a conversation in a comfortable environment, trusting that the one critiquing your work has your best interest at heart.

Critiquing Photographs

There are limitless ways photographers express themselves as we see with different eyes; therefore, there's countless ways of critiquing. Guidelines can be valuable for a clear, effective critique. While some people feel natural at critiquing, others might be comfortable following guidelines. A worthy critique remains friendly, thoughtful, positive, considerate and honest. Use proper etiquette, heartfelt responses, while showing another perspective.

Begin by finding positive aspects that work. Understand the sensitivity involved in critiquing, being aware and careful when phrasing responses.

Critique guidelines can be helpful in a group setting or for self-editing. Usually I begin with the emotional aspect because it's my first reaction that's felt in my heart.

1. <u>Emotional</u> - What was your immediate reaction.

> Note your impression and why. How does it grab your attention? Does it tell a story, feel familiar, arouse your imagination?

> For example:

> *This remind me of...,*

> *You seemed to have captured...*

> *It's a beautiful image because...*

If the image does NOT give a good first impression, you might respond:

I want to feel more…

I am trying to grasp the mood, the subject, the focal point, etc.

What were your thoughts behind this image?

Have you thought about a stronger impact by…

2. Artistic – Is the Composition simple, unique and memorable.

Is there a creative perspective? Is there a strong center of interest? Are there distractions that can be removed for stronger composition (branches, trees, people, dust, parts non-discernable)? Are the visual elements uniquely arranged?

We might Critique:

The composition might be more compelling if…

My eye is searching for…

If the subject were moved a little to the…. it might create…

If the subject were moved closer...or further away...

The angle of the subject might have more impact if...
The foreground/background is distracting, perhaps try...
For stronger impact, I would crop...
Tell me about the blur...

3. <u>Technical</u> – Does the exposure work

There's a fine line for technical quality, but the overall image's strength will determine good or bad technical skills.

Is there a range of dark and light, shadows and highlights? Is the image muddy with no contrast? Is the photo in focus or meant to be blurry? Is Photoshop overly used (colors too saturated, sharpness, contrast, brightness)?

We might Critique:

The image is dark, light, too muddy, I would change/add...

The highlights/shadows are...

The subject seems soft...

The sharp background adds/distracts

Actual Critique Sessions

Below are conversations from willing participants. The goal is to empower more people to critique and be critiqued.

JF: The bus shot has some unique style aspects to it. I like how you framed the image at an angle and how it was cropped, adding uniqueness. There's a story to be told here. I am left to wonder what the story is and why it's at an angle. I wonder about the lower right corner that my eye is drawn to. Perhaps darken that area a bit more to remove the distraction or brighten it if part of the story.

Photographer: *I see what you mean by the lower right hand corner. It is a street trashcan. There is more of a story in the image, one of transportation, moving people. I've reworked the image darkening out the trash. It looks much better.*

JF: The fashion shoot is technically good but has aspects in composition that can use tweaking. Fashion shoots are very detailed oriented, with styling assistance. To make it more fashion forward, I have some suggestions:

For more impact I might have had her looking directly into the mirror, being the camera's main focal point.

Her left arm is awkwardly placed

Styling issue, unless the back is part of the design element of the dress and important detail to photograph, I would cover her partial skin showing, as it's a distraction.

A line cuts through her neck, cutting the image in half.

Her make-up is severe. It could date the overall affect, instead of creating a more natural look. If you do more fashion shoots, I recommend glancing through high-end fashion magazines such as Vogue, Elle, studying the images, models and the overall composition.

Photographer: *The images of Julee (second time I've shot her) are the first time I've attempted "fashion shooting." The real professionals make it look so easy, well it isn't!! Julee would like to be a model, but she is tough to work with, she is a sweet gal, but has only one expression, the one you see and I can't get her to move to feel free. So my thought was to add something into the image to change things up some. I didn't think of* *having her look into the window and shooting her reflection. That would have been a great idea.*

As far as the dress and make-up it was her choice. I thought a bit heavy on the make-up. I wanted to darken the dress as you suggested but she didn't like that idea. I see what you mean with the left arm, I must be more aware of everything. The background line, I couldn't make up my mind to leave or take-out, I know now!!!

Your suggestion of picking up Vogue or Elle magazine and studying the images is a great one. I have been doing research on the web, but your suggestion is better. I'll also mention it to Julee, I believe it will help her as well.

JF: The image of the people walking on the pier at sunset is a great idea. I like the angle too, feeling like it's coming from your perspective. A few things to keep in mind while capturing what is a tough shot technically, aiming directly at the brightest subject that exists. Obviously you want the subjects who are walking to have detail so you expose midway between the sun and the subjects to capture both. Also bright lights in any situation will attract the eye. So as to avoid that, the subject needs to stand out more. My eye is also looking for the main focal point. Is it the people walking or is it the sun? The lines of infinity on the pier could have more impact if corners were involved, creating leading lines to the sun. Have one of the pier edges (right lower) touching a corner, even if it means angling the image a little more. Our goal is to have images with impact, an interesting focal point, clarity of subject (s) and of course pleasing to the eye.

Photographer: *I guess I've kind of over done the "not straight" concept and was thinking that "a cool, non-straight image* *with a big sun in it" would be a winner. Now after reading what you've said, I have to agree there is no one main focal point to the image, no story, not even a hint of one with the family in the middle, because of so many other people in the image. As been pointed out many times, it's okay to break the rules, if there is a reason and it works.*

JF: Great subject. Nice light and a subtle, interesting lit background. In this situation, my first approach would be to talk to him. Ask questions about his life, and have him tell his story. At the same time snap images, close ups and full body. I would be the one moving while continuing the dialogue. The viewer might crave to see more of him. Perhaps close ups with eye contact, as the eyes express a life led, and surely he's had an interesting one with much to say. Seeing his eyes might just be the spark that makes this image stand out a lot more. As much as I like this photo, him looking down with a smile isn't giving me enough information into his life while at the same time wondering what he's looking at. When shooting interesting subjects, show the viewer something of a life led, through the eyes and the body language. If you have someone with you, snap away while they are engaging with him.

JF: I happen to love this airport image. There is mystery in the darkness, from the technical way this image was shot. We want to know who she is, where she is going and where she is coming from. In this situation, we have only one time to get it right, as this moment is all we're given. The image is successful in capturing a story, and the movement shows the transition of the subject, and why we ask the questions, wanting to know more. I often set my camera at a background I like. Since someone will eventually walk where you'd expect, you're there ready. I wait for the right subject and snap at exactly where I want them.

JF: What is most interesting in this image is that his white apron stands out from the background. That works and possibly what caught your eye in the first place. Again, in this situation, I would have photographed every move he made just to get that one thing he does that's the winner pose, and most appealing to the eye. Experiment more with subject placement, further off center, when it just might be that little shift that gives it more visual impact. If you stayed with him, and nothing more happened, then this might be one of those images that end up in my 3 star file when grading in Lightroom (5 stars best, 4 stars maybe). Sometimes we find an image that catches our eye, but the end result comes out less interesting.

JF: This photo has a story. As a viewer, we just want to know more. She is closing the door, so we assume the horse is inside after a ride, perhaps just a practice. There are many ribbons on the door, which could be from her endeavors or not. She's the main subject. Who is she? Is she tired after winning or is she feeling sad from a loss. The viewer is left curious while wanting to feel some emotion. When photographing people doing their passion, an important angle is capturing the energy in regards to the activity.

Why Get Critiqued?

1. Find out what is and is not working, creating better images
2. Understand how to use simple post processing tools for strong, impactful images
3. Learn to self-edit
4. Uncover your style and passion, be inspired to get out and photograph with a clearer direction
5. Your vision expands, reproducing a masterpiece in the viewfinder from what you see in your surroundings

On a personal note: *Many years ago I experienced a Portfolio Review in Texas from an owner of a well-known gallery. It was a last minute decision to go with friends who were more experienced than I. A portfolio was created with my favorite B/W images. He said I had a great eye, however, it felt more like a bashing session of my random images. Looking back, I have to agree, there was no cohesiveness. But I left torn about a future in photography. His cold, insensitive remarks affected me. I wish I had a private critique prior to jumping into such a serious situation. The opposite approach was what I purposely implemented as a teacher, to support students in advancing their skills whatever their goals might be. I find something valuable and positive while getting more detailed into each image. I remain sensitive with a caring tone, offer suggestions, asking a lot of questions and always leave them inspired.*

http://sundaysinny.com/critique

THE CAMERA AS HEALER

A personal note

Traveling to remote lands in the back of a moving vehicle with camera in hand has always been liberating for me, and how my love affair with it first began. Other than my grown boys, life has not presented itself with any other *gifts* that come close to the purity of satisfaction I feel from this creative and inspiring calling.

I am fearless with camera in hand.

Having grown up shy, the camera empowered me and I transformed. I could walk into any event and talk to strangers. I could photograph well-known musicians in the 60's and 70's before and after concerts. None of this would remotely be possible without a camera around my neck.

It's that powerful.

The camera became my security and my protector. It has the incredible challenge and capacity to stop a moment in time that never presents itself again. And when I've captured the moment, I am deeply elated and extremely exhilarated.

The gratification is therapeutic.

For just around the corner is yet another hidden and exciting challenge that awakens my soul, reminding me just how alive I am!

With so little time to capture the slightest essence of a subject, I often concentrate on the eyes, where their story is told. Who are these people? What kind of lives have they led? What are their challenges, fears and joys?

When I capture the intimacy of a subject's memory, their pain, their secrets, their dreams, their quests, I also grow. I touch them in their loneliness, making sense just how deeply layered we all are.

For it is not by mere chance or accident that I am of equal vulnerability, photographing all parts of myself.

ABOUT JUDITH

Judith's photographic journey began at her first workshop with Ansel Adams and Yousuf Karsh in the 70's. She's worked as a photojournalist for newspapers in California and NYC, with her photos appearing in magazines and books worldwide. She used her press pass to photograph famous musicians such as Joan Baez, Kenny Loggins, Bonnie Raitt, Bob Marley, Al Jarreau, etc, at the local arena. Judith traveled extensively around the world working for airlines such as Pan Am, TWA, Iberia Air, Air Moroc. She was also co-founder and creator of the first online member based educational photographic website in the early 90's (photoworkshop.com).

For the past 10 years, she's concentrated on teaching *The Art of Seeing*, specializing in perfecting photo composition to all ages and levels in places such as China, with the Tibetan students in Dharamsala, India, workshops in Mexico and with Australian students, to her popular *Sundays in NY* street photography workshops in New York City. Any camera format is welcome (plus the iPhone only sessions). She's also passionate about and expert in critiquing photographer's images for quick improvement while leading small groups and private sessions online. Her expertise and professional guidance expedites improvement of the photographer's eye. Her enthusiasm to inspire forever changes those who have experienced her sessions.

Judith's personal passion is in environmental portraits, finding special moments of energy while achieving perfect framing. Her images portray simple folk in their day-to-day rituals showing the spirit and flavor of a culture, from the warmth of their faces to the simplicity of the composition.

When she's not traveling, Judith spends her time in New York City and Todos Santos, Baja California Sur, Mexico.

Portfolio: judithfarber.com
Teaching: Sundaysinny.com
Instagram: instagram.com/sundaysinewyork

25523239R00060

Printed in Poland
by Amazon Fulfillment
Poland Sp. z o.o., Wrocław